# Minute Men and Women

# Minute Men and Women

Poems by

Anne Waters Green

© 2021 Anne Waters Green. All rights reserved.
This material may not be reproduced in any form, published,
reprinted, recorded, performed, broadcast,
rewritten or redistributed without
the explicit permission of Anne Waters Green.
All such actions are strictly prohibited by law.

Cover Art: composite designed by Landon Westbrook from the following photos: 1937 photograph of the poet's parents on their honeymoon by an unknown street photographer, istock.com/JackF, and Annie Spratt on Unsplash.

Back cover headshot by Sarah Kohut.

ISBN: 978-1-63980-058-2

Kelsay Books
502 South 1040 East, A-119
American Fork, Utah 84003
Kelsaybooks. com

*Look to the rock from which you were cut, and to the quarry from which you were hewn.*
—Isaiah 51:1b

This book is dedicated to my quarry: all those, known and unknown, who went before and whose lives and loves contributed to my being.

And especially to my rocks: my parents, Thomas Landon Waters (1908–2007) and Dorothy Lee Allen Waters (1915–2009). Their love and encouragement sustain me still.

# Acknowledgments

This book of poems would not exist but for the warm encouragement of Cathy Smith Bowers and Dr. Ken Chamlee, exquisite poets and teachers extraordinaire. Cathy introduced me to the minute form. After reading the first few minutes, Ken suggested they might be the start of a chapbook. A minute is a 60 syllable poem written in three 20 syllable stanzas, each consisting of an 8 syllable line followed by three 4 syllable lines. The rhyme scheme is aa, bb, cc, dd, ee, ff.

I am grateful to my poetry sisters, Jane Mary Curran, Karen Luke Jackson, and Emily Wilmer. Their suggestions, both sharp and gentle, have improved these and other poems—what a gift their friendship has been.

My sisters, Dottie Bryan and Peggy Rowland, and my daughters, Landon Westbrook and Anne Allen Westbrook have listened to many of these stories in much longer versions for decades. I thank them for their patience. The subjects of these poems are their people too.

It is a joy to share life with my husband, Jim, also an amateur genealogist. I am especially fortunate to have him as first reader, travel companion, and breakfast cook.

The following poems appeared in *Great Smokies Review,* Vol. 17, Fall 2017.

"Rebecca Gibson Starnes Recalls Her Role In Witch Hunting"

"James Hollis Tells His Life Story To His Grandchildren"

"Landon Waters Remembers How His Father Died"

"Jeremiah Allen Works To Warm His Home"

"Aunt Shady Mourns A Lost Generation"

Also by Anne Waters Green *The Season Lengthens*

# Contents

| | |
|---|---:|
| Rebecca Gibson Starnes Admits Her Role In Witch-Hunting | 13 |
| Gabriel Baubeau Leaves Questions In His Wake | 14 |
| Elizabeth Spencer White Baubeau Persists | 15 |
| Charles Starnes Leaves Massachusetts | 16 |
| Edward Musgrove Finds Himself And His Family In The Midst Of A Battle | 17 |
| Boardwine Waters I Tells Why He Got Locked Up In the Ninety Six Jail | 18 |
| Boardwine Waters I Gains Mercy | 19 |
| Joseph Wofford Introduces A Southern Political Tradition | 20 |
| Thomas Hill's Death Remains A Mystery | 21 |
| James Hollis Narrates His Life's Drama | 22 |
| Boardwine Waters II Explains Why He Sued John Farrow | 23 |
| Landon Waters I Remembers His Father's Sacrifice | 24 |
| Benjamin Wofford Founds A College | 25 |
| Thomas Willoughby Waters Makes His Choice At The Auction Of His Father's Estate | 26 |
| Thomas Willoughby Waters Chooses Cousin Hannah as Wife Number Two | 27 |
| John Phillips Keeps Farming Through The Civil War | 28 |
| Henry A. Allen Joins the Confederate Army and Dies of Dysentery at Fort Delaware | 29 |
| Sarah Phillips Allen Laments Her Husband's Absence | 30 |
| Aunt Shady Mourns A Lost Generation | 31 |
| Landon Waters II Pays The Price | 32 |

| | |
|---|---|
| William Wesley Stone and Ann Perotine Hollis Raise a Family | 33 |
| Martha Susan Layton Waters And Elmore Bishop Huff Unite In Marriage | 34 |
| Mary Frances Adams Snead Was Born On Independence Day | 35 |
| Jeremiah Solomon Allen Worked To Warm His Place | 36 |
| Louisa Louella Jones Allen Poses With Her Husband | 37 |
| Jesse Coleman Waters Remains A Puzzle To The Granddaughters He Never Knew | 38 |
| Mamie Stone Waters' Granddaughter Considers A Photograph | 39 |
| Henry Arthur Allen Shows His Mettle | 40 |
| Maude Anne Snead Allen Sets Her Course Early | 41 |
| Thomas Landon Waters Grows Up In A Small South Carolina Town | 42 |
| The Poet's Parents Visit The National's Capital | 43 |
| Tom Waters Devises A Plan | 44 |
| Tom Waters Avoids Lung Cancer But Does Not Escape | 45 |
| Dorothy Lee Allen Waters Remembers Her Father's Encouragement | 46 |
| Dot Waters Delivers Her Second Daughter In 1941 | 47 |
| The Poet Places Her Birth In History | 48 |
| The Breech Baby Becomes A Poet | 49 |
| The Poet Salutes Her Ancestors | 50 |

# Rebecca Gibson Starnes Admits Her Role In Witch-Hunting

(1635–1681)


Yes, I did. I called them witches,
had a vision
neighbor lady
hexed my baby.

I pointed at her daughter too,
felt such a queue
of emotions
and wild notions.

I regret father paid a fine.
The fault was mine.
I slandered them,
my words mayhem.

# Gabriel Baubeau Leaves Questions In His Wake

(c. 1651–1737)


Tell us more, Gabriel Baubeau.
At first, you show
in Virginia,
wed a widow,

father her son, then disappear.
For sure, our fear
was that you died
before your time.

But you turned up in Maryland,
new wife, new son.
Sit and tarry,
spill your story.

# Elizabeth Spencer White Baubeau Persists

(c. 1682–1726)

Her first spouse died, the Frenchman left
Elizabeth
but she trod on,
raised her sons,

worked her estate, even signed deeds.
Which of life's creeds
did she obey?
We cannot say.

We celebrate a woman strong
who sang her song,
showed fortitude,
stood resolute.

# Charles Starnes Leaves Massachusetts

(c. 1702–1778)


Four generations of my clan
in New England
and I was first
to take the risk,

move far down south to Charlestowne
where soon I found
Ann Fogarty.
Matrimony

followed. Five sturdy sons were born.
Like Abraham's,
my progeny
now are many.

# Edward Musgrove Finds Himself And His Family In The Midst Of A Battle

(1730–1796)


I, a surveyor, after all,
saw Horseshoe Falls,
knew I could build
a fine grist mill

and home, dwell 'neath my own fig tree.
My family
was large, third wife
young, full of life.

I worried when the Tory hoard
camped in my yard,
bringing battle
to Musgrove's Mill.

# Boardwine Waters I Tells Why He Got Locked Up In the Ninety Six Jail

(1736–1781)

I was down to the store with no
damn intent to
pick a fight. That
blamed Tory rat

pulled a weapon on me, said he'd
shoot myself dead
unless I swore
an oath before

all to join the king's side. I wasn't
a Loyalist,
so grabbed his gun.
Shot him just once.

# Boardwine Waters I Gains Mercy

(1736–1781)


Funny what Brother Phil advised
me to do. Said
"turn yourself in."
Soon as I did,

he came with some fellows. They broke
me out, but, folks,
the story's not
done. I still got

convicted of murder.  Later
legislature
heard my plea.  Won
me a pardon.

# Joseph Wofford Introduces A Southern Political Tradition

(1742–1831)


Low country planters and clergy
rode up-country;
they sought our might
to join the fight,

whip up on the Tory menace.
Independence,
the stated goal.
I chose the role

of welcoming host, roasted meat
for all to eat
the day I threw
a barbeque.

# Thomas Hill's Death Remains A Mystery

(c. 1750–1826)

When George the Third granted acreage
Thomas Hill scored
a tract close by
the Enoree's

north shore, a place to make a home
for daughters, sons,
wife. Joined the fight
for self-rule rights.

None now know why this strong man chose
to use a noose
to quell his breath,
to beckon death.

# James Hollis Narrates His Life's Drama

(1757–1847)


I was born in Wandsworth Surrey
took a journey
as a soldier
of old King George.

After the Siege at Ninety Six,
I up and slipped
away. My fife
and I made life

among the rebels. My story:
once a Tory,
heart enshrined in
Carolina.

# Boardwine Waters II Explains Why He Sued John Farrow

(1761–1820)


I know I'm John's own cousin, not
his woman's but
she was the one
needing aid from

a man. The law calls such "next friend."
That scoundrel John
took up with her
younger sister,

threatened to sell the home place where
his Mary fared
with their large brood.
I helped her sue.

# Landon Waters I Remembers His Father's Sacrifice

(1764–1827)


Uncle Phil raised the regiment;
my father went
and I did too.
We never knew

what would transpire. I saw Tory
blackguards shoot my
father dead mere
minutes after

he'd made a deal to free me from
them. I'd been plumb
afraid I'd die.
Instead, he did.

# Benjamin Wofford Founds A College

(1780–1850)


Canny old Uncle Ben Wofford
preached God's Word,
farmed his acreage.
The man died rich.

His will left money to found an
institution
for high study.
His legacy

stuns still—among the largest pledged
for a college
those years before
the Civil War.

# Thomas Willoughby Waters Makes His Choice At The Auction Of His Father's Estate

(1801–1858)

Father attained sizable wealth
before his death
in '22.
Surely he knew

to write a will. Because he didn't,
it was a given
to hold a sale.
Vigorous male

of nineteen years, my heart's desire
was very clear:
to bid and snare
father's bay mare.

# Thomas Willoughby Waters Chooses Cousin Hannah as Wife Number Two

(1801–1858)  (1809–1846)


Hannah Waters was her husband's
mate, his cousin
too, their fathers
were full brothers.

Thomas Waters had wed before.
His first had borne
two babes, then died.
This second bride

birthed three, two sons and a daughter.
Tom wept for her
when death appeared.
Soon chose the third.

# John Phillips Keeps Farming Through The Civil War

(1812–1868)

I was old for army duty.
My able boy
signed up. My lame
son and I aimed

to keep the crops a-growing as
we could. Neighbors
bought four cotton
bales, paid me in

worthless Southern dollars. They knew
Lee'd surrendered.
I took those men
to court and won.

# Henry A. Allen Joins the Confederate Army and Dies of Dysentery at Fort Delaware

(1830–1865)

Henry Allen marched off to war.
Whatever for?
Owned no slaves, not
even land, but

something convinced him to sign on.
Wish he had known
the cause was fraught.
Destiny caught

him at Wilderness. He died in
Union prison.
Heartbroken wife
for their lost life.

# Sarah Phillips Allen Laments Her Husband's Absence

(1833–1870)


Henry's brother wrote the letter.
Fiery fever
had me too weak.
*You ought to seek*

*a train ride home. Your family*
*hungers to see*
*your face. Your wife*
*scarce clings to life.*

*Your baby girl has died.* That word
was true. I burned
with grief. What cost,
all we had lost.

# Aunt Shady Mourns A Lost Generation

(1840–1918)


My own brothers went off to war.
Will died in far
off Elmira,
a prisoner.

Young Landon survived Point Lookout,
wed, had two stout
sons, was lucky
he got to see

home again. Many young men lost.
I felt the cost.
Both my husbands—
old widowers.

# Landon Waters II Pays The Price

(1843–1881)

Landon Waters joined up to fight
Yankees whose might
was great. Captured
but with breath spared

he suffered at the marshy damp
Point Lookout camp.
The man limped home
when war was done.

Married Miss Layton, sired three sons.
With weakened lungs
soon death his fate
at thirty-eight.

# William Wesley Stone and Ann Perotine Hollis Raise a Family

(1844–1926)             (1854–1933)


"Billy" Stone, home from war, wed Miss
"Tiney" Hollis,
sired six daughters.
They all shed tears

when the next baby, a boy, died.
Shoulders squared,
the two endured.
Was joy restored

when one last little girl arrived?
Was she too prized
like a bonny
son might have been?

# Martha Susan Layton Waters And Elmore Bishop Huff Unite In Marriage

(1848–1930)          (1847–1922)

Miz Martha needed a second
husband. Elmore
wanted a wife.
They joined their lives

and families, her sons, his girls
and boys. Fate hurls
curves at each of
us. Was it love

or convenience when widower
and sad widow
each chose anew
to say "I do?"

# Mary Frances Adams Snead Was Born On Independence Day

(1854–1936)


She traveled on horseback to wed
Will Snead. They led
a simple life,
she fertile wife—

he farmer man. Offspring numbered
fifteen. They cleared
land, planted seed
to grow their food.

For her birthday, the Fourth of July,
Will always tried
to ripen one
watermelon.

# Jeremiah Solomon Allen Worked To Warm His Place

(1857–1883)


The ax was great-grandfather's tool
for stacking fuel
to warm the farm—
house, wife and bairn.

Swinging that blade he sliced his shin.
The open skin
drew dirt, bred rot.
Fierce hope could not

freeze the fatal slide toward death.
He left bereft
his wife who wept,
their babe who slept.

# Louisa Louella Jones Allen Poses With Her Husband

(1861–1891)


Your portrait hangs on my bedroom
wall. You, your groom
both look so young,
lives just begun.

Your belly's slight curve announces
a baby is
soon to be born.
Fate did not warn

how closely joy and grief can cleave
together, weave
a baby's birth,
with husband's death.

# Jesse Coleman Waters Remains A Puzzle To The Granddaughters He Never Knew

(1877–1951)

Would we understand if we knew
more about you?
Your father died,
Ma remarried,

Aunt took younger brother under
her wing. Wonder
how you fared? We,
granddaughters three,

know that you left your only son,
your wife, were done
with family.
Was life carefree?

# Mamie Stone Waters' Granddaughter Considers A Photograph

(1882–1936)

The picture gives much to admire—
glossy dark hair,
intricate lace
collar, strong face.

Your steady gaze does not reveal
the anguish felt
when your husband
broke off loving

you, left you with a son to raise.
Did you always
mask emotions,
rein in passion?

# Henry Arthur Allen Shows His Mettle

(1882–1946)


The newspaper columnist called
your voice a drawl
when he heard you
start to argue

in court, deliberate and slow.
Did he not know
your peers at bar
thought you stellar,

a lawyer's lawyer whose warm heart
belied the smart
ways you carried
home a jury.

# Maude Anne Snead Allen Sets Her Course Early

(1887–1981)


Maude, middle child, seven older,
seven younger.
Pa's favorite
because the sight

of her straight furrows made him proud.
This daughter sowed
so carefully.
Her strict esprit

held true as lawyer's wife, mother
to five, lover
of home, garden.
Stoic Spartan.

## Thomas Landon Waters Grows Up In A Small South Carolina Town

(1908–2007)


His dad took off for New Orleans,
left his son genes—
good looks, height, charm—
and lasting shame—

most boys of his time had fathers
at home. Yet he
thrived. Boys wanted him
on all their teams.

When their mothers needed a fourth for
bridge, they soon found
he had card sense.
His place was cinched.

# The Poet's Parents Visit The National's Capital

Thomas Landon Waters (1908–2007) and Dorothy Lee Allen (1915–2009)

On their honeymoon the newly-
weds tour D.C.
They're young, in love,
the girl wears gloves.

The man bought a new fedora.
A sleek aura
surrounds the pair,
enough to lure

an eager street photographer's
eye. Camera
flashes: the moment
in time frozen.

# Tom Waters Devises A Plan

(1908–2007)

King of his own small domain, he
had one wife, three
daughters. His mild
joke: some girl child

was in the bathroom any time
that nature chimed.
His main request
for the new house:

one loo for all the women, and
one just for men,
No need to share
since no male heir.

# Tom Waters Avoids Lung Cancer But Does Not Escape

(1908–2007)

All the fellows smoked tobacco,
the thing to do
for boys in the
1920s.

Cigarettes for decades, then right
to lighting pipes.
Peril to his
life? Cancer was

not his fate. Arthritic hands dropped
the match. Flames snapped.
Our mighty oak
went down in smoke.

# Dorothy Lee Allen Waters Remembers Her Father's Encouragement

(1915–2009)

She loved to tell about dinner
debates. Older
siblings scoffed at
her remarks but

their father scolded: "She has a right
to shine her light
just as you do."
It's the truth

that's how this daddy's girl
learned so well
that her own views
had value too.

# Dot Waters Delivers Her Second Daughter In 1941

(1915–2009)

While laboring my mother heard
the doctor's word
"breech" voiced aloud.
She whispered "scared."

Without anesthesia, birthed me
not head, not feet,
but fanny first
I tore and burst

from her warm womb into this world.
Small limbs unfurled,
new born lungs stirred
to gulp sweet air.

# The Poet Places Her Birth In History

(1941–)


Born a South Carolina girl
just before Pearl
Harbor. Neither
baby boomer

nor war baby, instead Silent
Generation,
Great Depression
conceived, a sign

parents hoped for a fresh era.
Only lovers
seeing the light
would bear new life.

# The Breech Baby Becomes A Poet

(1941–)

My birth an omen?  Maybe so.
If you must know
I could tantrum
with the best of them.

But here's more truth. Ugly duckling
became fledgling
swan, studied law.
married, bore two

daughters, divorced. Career, bar and
bench.  New husband
and poetry
tender much joy.

# The Poet Salutes Her Ancestors

I salute you, keepers of flames,
grantors of names,
genes, traditions.
You farmed, sired sons

birthed daughters. Some put down roots,
a few footloose.
Men marched to war
wives stoked home fires.

You sliced watermelons and threw
big bar-b-ques.
Love, joy, courage—
my heritage.

# About the Author

After a long career as a lawyer and later administrative judge, Anne Waters Green finds joy in reading and writing poetry and in genealogical research. She and her husband, Jim, are grandparents to a combined total of ten grandchildren whose visits and antics make for busy summers. After many years in the mountains of western North Carolina, where they enjoyed the parade of deer, wild turkeys, and other wildlife across their yard, they have recently returned to the Georgia coast.

www.ingramcontent.com/pod-product-compliance
Lightning Source LLC
Chambersburg PA
CBHW021028090426
42738CB00007B/936